THE CROSS
BEFORE
CALVARY

THE CROSS
BEFORE CALVARY

Clovis G. Chappell

ABINGDON PRESS
NEW YORK • NASHVILLE

THE CROSS BEFORE CALVARY

Library of Congress Catalog Card Number: 60-12070

SET UP, PRINTED, AND BOUND BY THE
PARTHENON PRESS, AT NASHVILLE,
TENNESSEE, UNITED STATES OF AMERICA

To my nephew,
the *REV. THOMAS HYDE CHAPPELL,*
whose brief and brilliant ministry
now continues on life's other side.

Contents

THE CROSS
BEFORE CALVARY

"God chose him to fulfill his part before the world was founded."—I Pet. 1:20 (Phillips)

The part that our Lord was chosen to fulfill was none other than the redemption of the world by his death on the Cross. Thus this text takes us back into the eternities. The crucifixion of our Savior is of course a fact of time. He was put to death on a certain hill at a certain date. But if this cross is a fact of time, it is also a fact of eternity. Calvary makes visible before our eyes what our Lord suffers now and what he has always suffered since that dateless day that he decided to dare the infinite risk of rearing a human family.

The startling fact that God suffers in our suffering was an insight of a few of the greatest of the prophets. "In all their affliction he was afflicted." Among these was Hosea. He saw it through his own bitter tears. The woman he loved proved unfaithful. She deserted him, shamed him, wrecked his home. But though forgotten, it was his hell that he could not forget. He could neither dust the soiled creature off his hands nor cast her out of his heart. Thus he suffered in her sufferings and wept in her tears.

It was as he brooded over his own betrayal by Gomer

9

that it came home to him that God had been betrayed far more tragically than himself. Therefore, as he suffered in the sin and shame of his prodigal wife, even so God must suffer in the sin of his prodigal children. Not only so, but he was sure that God's suffering was as much greater than his own as God was greater than himself. Thus this prophet, with eyes washed bright by tears, came to see a cross on the heart of God long before that cross became visible on Golgotha.

I

We can glimpse some understanding of this when we realize that our Lord's life did not begin at his birth. He had been from the beginning. "In the beginning was the Word, and the Word was with God, and the Word was God." When he reached the end of his earthly journey, he, and he alone, could offer this prayer: "Father, glorify thou me in thy own presence with the glory which I had with thee before the world was made."

Since our Lord had known the glory and joy of the intimate presence of God from eternity, it is not surprising that he knew joy as a citizen of our world. To think of Jesus as a gloomy man is, in my opinion, to be vastly wrong. He was a sunny man. He was a man who could laugh and sing. So true was this that he often shocked the rock-ribbed religionists of his day.

They could easily accept John the Baptist as a religious man. He wore a hair shirt, lived on a diet of locust and wild honey, and never attended any kind of feast. But Jesus was the opposite. He never, so far as the record goes, refused an invitation to dinner. He delighted in human companionship, even that of outcasts. He was at home at weddings. Therefore, the sour saints of his day did not regard him as a religious man, but rather as a glutton, a wine-bibber, and a friend of folks that were no more than worthless riffraff.

If Jesus offended these grim saints by what he did, he offended them equally by what he said. He often had such queer words as these upon his lips. "Happy are the poor in spirit; joyful are the merciful; oh the gladness of the pure in heart!" Not only so, but he said all this with the solid sincerity that could come only from experience. Even little children so felt the contagion of his joy that they found him irresistible. Therefore, they often fought their way out of their own mothers' arms to climb into his. Children seldom struggle to get into the lap of a thundercloud.

Other words that our Lord had upon his lips again and again were these: "Be of good cheer." He said this to one who had made himself a hopeless cripple by his own wrong doing. "Be of good cheer, your sins are forgiven you." He also said this great word as he faced the disaster of the Cross. "Be of good cheer, I have overcome the world." We may be sure that the cheer which he offered to others was carried in his own heart. We may also be sure that the cheer which he knew here was known even more fully before our world was born.

But if Jesus knew laughter, he also knew tears. A man of his tenderness could not live in a world like ours without suffering a broken heart. He was a man of sorrows and acquainted with grief. Those who knew this sunny Savior best were doubtless a bit shocked by his tears. They never forgot how he wept by the grave of his friend Lazarus. Not often was he so deeply moved.

But if his disciples were surprised at his tears by the grave of his friend, they were later horrified at hearing him sob aloud—and that, as they thought, at the hour of his supreme triumph. He was making his way toward Jerusalem. Everybody was delirious with joy. The King was at last going to receive his crown. Then came that terribly discordant note. Somebody was sobbing aloud. But most shocking of all, that somebody was none other than the King himself. "He beheld the city, and wept over it." By the grave of Lazarus he wept softly. Here he sobbed aloud.

That Jesus was a man both of laughter and tears is not surprising. He would not have been truly human if this had not been the case. A gentleman speaking of his pastor commended him for the fact that he never made any hearer either laugh or cry. I could not join him in his enthusiasm. I could only remember that the last dummy I had seen in a show window affected me the same way. It stirred me neither to laughter nor tears. It left me as unmoved as itself.

In affirming that our Lord was a man who knew both joy and sorrow, I am sure that the note of joy was predominant. We are to remember also that he was joyous not so much in spite of the Cross as because of the Cross. We read that when he took the cup, the cup that signified life laid down, he gave thanks. Surely this was more than a formal asking of the blessing; it was a pouring out of his gratitude to the Father for the privilege of giving himself for our redemption. When he went out to the loneliness of Geth-

semane, he went with a song on his lips. When certain
women sobbed over him on his way to Calvary, he told them
that it was not he but they and their children who were the
tragic actors in this bloody drama. Indeed, if we may believe
that quotation from the writer to the Hebrews, the face of
Jesus was the sunniest that ever looked upon our world.
"Therefore God, thy God, has annointed thee with the oil
of gladness beyond thy comrades." He, therefore, knew
laughter and tears, but laughter I repeat was predominant.

Lu 23: 26f

Heb 1:9

II

Yet when our Lord disclosed the Cross to his friends, they
were shocked and repelled. In indignation Simon could
only say, "God forbid." "You are right," he is affirming,
"in seeking to save the world, but to seek this goal by madly
throwing your life away on a cross is unthinkable."

But our Lord did not commend his friend for this
seductive word. He rather gave him about the sharpest
rebuke that he ever gave to a disciple. "Out of my way
Satan; you are not talking the language of God but of
Satan himself. In the wilderness Satan boldly offered to
give me the kingdoms of the world if I would only bypass
Calvary. But this I cannot do." Then he added, "Not only
is the Cross a necessity for me but for you as well. Indeed,
it is impossible for anyone to be my disciple except at the
cost of the Cross."

What did Jesus mean? What is it to bear the Cross?
Some regard the Cross as any load that life may lay upon
our shoulders. I am thinking of a friend who suffered a
great sorrow. Her only daughter, a girl of rare beauty, was

marred and scarred by a horrible disease. This mother became so bitter that I felt powerless to help her, though I was both her pastor and friend. Her attitude was this: "God had no right to take my child, no right to lay upon me such a ghastly cross." But her grief was not in reality a cross; it was only a galling and tormenting burden.

What, I repeat, is the Cross? It is a burden that we take upon ourselves voluntarily. That was what the Cross meant to Jesus. He had arrayed against him a handful of the shrewdest of politicians. It would be hard to find a more cunning and cruel group than that headed by Annas. This group was able to bring powerful pressure upon Pilate. In spite of the fact that this official had a certain sense of justice, his supreme ambition was to keep his position. Therefore, he allowed these shrewd priests so to manipulate him that he had little more choice of what he would do or say than the dummy of a ventriloquist.

But these enemies, keen and cruel as they were, had not the power to bring about our Lord's death. He, himself, affirmed that he was not the victim of foes who were too strong for him. Determined as they were, they did not wrench life out of his clinging hands and gripping fingers. Our Lord plainly affirms the opposite. "No one takes it (my life) from me, but I lay it down of my own accord." If we, by bearing the Cross, become disciples, it must be by our own choice.

But while it is true that the Cross is not any load that life may lay upon us, it is also true that any load may become a cross and exercise the lifting power of a cross, provided we learn to accept and bear it within the will of

God. There is a parable that says that once the birds had no wings. God threw wings at their feet and commanded them to lift and to bear them against their own breasts. This they did, at first with bitterness. But by and by, as they held these wings close to their hearts, they grew there. Thus what was once only a load became a lifting power. A kindred experience may be ours.

In imagination I slipped recently into a little service of the long ago. A certain man named Simon, an African, stood and gave this testimony:

Years ago, as a proselyte, I went from Cyrene to attend the great feast at Jerusalem. Early on a fateful Friday morning I hurried toward the city from the home of a friend where I had spent the night. To my amazement when I came near Jerusalem, the crowds were headed out of the city, instead of into it. Asking what this meant, I was told that three prisoners were that day to pay the death penalty.

I had never witnessed an execution, so I decided I would look at the gruesome sight, at least as long as I could bear it. I was especially eager to see the men who were doomed to die. So being a husky chap, I elbowed my way through the crowd until I was near enough to have touched the prisoners with my own hand. Two of them were vigorous men, rough, sinewy, and hard as nails. The other, while a fine figure of a man, was evidently suffering from much blood letting. Indeed he was so weakened that even as I looked, his knees buckled and he fell under the weight of his cross.

Then the ghastly thing happened! A strong hand gripped my shoulder, a short sword flashed in the sun, and a voice of authority thundered at me, "You there, take up that cross." Going hot and cold, I was on the point of refusing. I felt that

I could not have heard right. But there was no mistake. Therefore, with a curse on my lips and rage in my heart I shouldered the hated load and fell in beside the man whose burden I had taken.

This man, so far as I remember, said never a word to me. But the very breath of him somehow cooled the hot fires of my resentment. Even by his silence he seemed to say, "I am sorry to have involved you in this, but I am not quite up to myself this morning." Then when we came to the foot of the hill he made as if he would take over. But to my utter amazement I heard myself say, "Never mind, I will be glad to carry it for you up the hill and all the way."

And carry it I did. I stood by and watched the grim work of crucifixion. I heard him pray for his enemies. I heard him when at last he dropped his tired and tortured body into the arms of eternal Love, praying, "Father into thy hands I commit my spirit." By all this he so completely won my heart that I took up his cross of my own choice. From that day to this what was once my shame has been my glory.

Thus we bear the Cross not only when we, of our own choice, for Christ's sake take upon ourselves the burdens of others, but also when we come to accept a once unwelcome burden gladly within his will and for his sake. That is the way of discipleship. This was true before Calvary became a historic fact. It has been true ever since. It will be true forevermore.

How long has it been since two times two began to make four? Really, it would be impossible to fix the date. When did it become true that it is more blessed to give than to receive? That didn't begin when Jesus said those words. It is eternally true; therefore, he said them. When the murderers of Jesus threw this taunt at him, "He saved others; he cannot save himself," that was true, but it did not become true because these men said it. Even so it would have been equally true had they said the opposite, "He saved himself; he cannot save others."

Therefore, this bearing of the Cross, without which there is no discipleship, no abundant life, is eternally essential. Those who experience its life-giving power belong to no particular day but to every day. We have a better opportunity to see and understand than did the men before Calvary. Yet its power was experienced by certain choice souls long before it was lifted upon that skull-shaped hill. Being sure of this, I am inviting you to sit with me at the feet of some of those who lived in the spirit of the Cross before Calvary. They also could sing, at least in spirit, along with us of today:

> O Cross that liftest up my head,
> I dare not ask to fly from Thee;
> I lay in dust life's glory dead,
> And from the ground there blossoms red
> Life that shall endless be.

17

FINDING THE BEST
THROUGH THE WORST—*Joseph*

> *"As for you, you meant evil against me;*
> *but God meant it for good."*—Gen. 50:20

■ Here is a scene to lift the heart. The sheer loveliness of it fairly makes us gasp. Joseph, who spoke these great words, has for a long time played his part well. But here he is at his beautiful best. Though already taller than the mountains, his height seems even greater in part because of the littleness of his whining brothers. They have come fawningly to ask forgiveness, and Joseph grants their request so magnificently that he reminds us of our Lord, as from his Cross he offered pardon to those who were doing him to death.

I

It is evident that Joseph had reached a great height. But he did not do so at a single bound. He had traveled a long and rugged road. Take a glance at the way along which he came.

1. The first glimpse we get of Joseph is in the tent of a nomad. He belongs to a family where there are four sets of children. Such a situation is never conducive to the greatest

harmony. He is the son of Jacob's favorite wife and is the youngest, except Benjamin, of his large family.

But in spite of his youth he is dressed better than his brothers. His father has given him quite a colorful coat. This was an offense in itself, but it was a yet greater offense because it meant that this younger brother was to become the leader of the clan. He was his father's favorite. That was not too good in itself. But, to make matters worse, Jacob openly showed his favoritism. If such a show of partiality was not good for the elder brothers, it was still worse for Joseph.

Of course, the fact that this teen-ager should be Jacob's favorite was almost inevitable. Not only was he the son of Rachel, the favorite wife, but he was far the handsomest and the brightest of the lot. In addition he was the possessor of both personality and charm.

Now knowing himself to be his father's favorite, he was not long in agreeing fully with his father and even surpassing him. This assurance that he was vastly superior to his cloddish brothers helped to set him to dreaming of his future greatness. That was not bad in itself, but it was bad that he was silly enough to tell those dreams to his brothers. Thus he flaunted his superiority in their faces. He further antagonized them by becoming a talebearer and reporting their ill conduct to father Jacob.

Thus it is evident that this promising youth, in spite of his ability, was in some respects quite foolish. He did not have imagination enough to put himself in the place of his brothers. He was too adolescent to consider their feelings. The fact that he loved himself better than he loved anybody else does not mean that he did not care at all for his brothers. He did. But being too full of himself, without thinking, he filled whole reservoirs of hate in the hearts of his brothers. That hatred resulted in a lot of hell for all concerned.

2. The second scene shows this hell in action. One day these brothers looked across the plain and saw an ostentatious and well-dressed swaggerer coming in their direction. "That's the dreamer," they said with bitter malice. So when this dreamer arrived, instead of receiving the expected welcome, he was greeted with hellish hate. With rough hands they tore off his colorful coat. Then they dropped him into a dry well where not a single star nor even a shock of wheat bowed to him. Here, facing death, he began in some measure to die to his own self-importance.

This would have been the end for Joseph except for the keen business instinct of his brother Judah. The sight of a company of merchants in the distance gave this schemer a happy thought. "Let us not kill our brother," he said in a tone that oozed unction, "lest his blood be on our hands. Instead let us sell him as a slave. Then we shall be guiltless; besides we shall be twenty dollars to the good." Of course, such an appeal for compassion was irresistible, and the sale was made.

There is no measuring the utter desperation and heartache with which this seventeen-year-old slave began his journey into the unknown. He could not have dreamed of a worse fate. But what made his crucifixion the more bitter was that it came at the hands of his own brothers whom he really loved and upon whose love he had foolishly counted.

But in spite of his hopeless situation this youth refused to give way to despair. Instead he said, "If I have to be a slave, I will be the best slave possible." Therefore, having become the property of one Potiphar, he began at once to take interest in all the interests of his master. Thus by being able and interested, he was soon the most trusted man in his master's household.

This led to further complications. Relations between the sexes in Egypt were even more lax than in America. Soon no less a personage than the wife of his master threw herself at him. Here he faced a chance to gather grapes of thorns or figs from thistles. But how grandly he won! "Can I do this great evil and sin against God?" What words from the lips of a slave whose own religious brothers had thrown him away!

What was his reward? Well, he got no medal, no promotion, instead he lost his position. He was cast into prison. But this, too, he faced without bitterness. He was learning to be interested in others. Here again by his ability, and by his determined friendliness, he was soon so trusted by his jailor that he became the most powerful man in the jail. Those in trouble turned to him naturally. Among them was an officer of Pharaoh who was then in disgrace. Joseph gave such timely help to this chap that the grateful man said he would never forget. But in spite of his pledge for many months he did forget.

Then when something prodded his dull memory, he spoke to the king of Joseph's ability. As a result the young prisoner was released. Not only so, but he was soon so trusted by Pharaoh that he was given a position of responsibility and honor. What was better still, he was by that time ready for his promotion. It did not make him a bundle of conceit as it might have done had it come to him sooner.

3. Now in this position of power Joseph was called upon to plan against future disaster. When starvation scourged his brothers into Egypt, Joseph sold them sufficient food to save their lives. Not only so, but he disclosed himself to them and promised them forgiveness. That forgiveness he showed by inviting them into Egypt and locating them in Goshen, the garden spot of the nation. Here they prospered in numbers and wealth till they became a force with which to reckon.

Then came for these brothers a final disaster. Jacob died. They had never believed that Joseph had really forgiven them. He had only delayed taking vengeance for their father's sake. Now that he was out of the way, they were sure that powerful Joseph would feed fat the ancient grudge he bore them. Therefore, they came to their exalted brother begging again for forgiveness.

II

Joseph's response we know. He did forgive, not grudgingly, but wholeheartedly. "Am I in the place of God?" he questions. We often think we are. We often dare to take matters in our own hands and exact vengeance for ourselves. But even in that distant day Joseph refused to usurp the throne of God.

How was he able to forgive so magnificently? Forgiveness is not always easy. That some of us know. Those words from Jesus that we are to forgive till seventy times seven would be positively crushing were it not a reminder that he who requires such forgiveness from us certainly will not do less himself.

But if forgiveness is not always easy, it is always an absolute essential. This is true whatever we may have suffered at the hands of another. Of all the cruel emotions that tear personality into shreds and tatters, none is quite equal to hate. My hate may not work the slightest harm to the one I hate, but it will certainly make hell for me. We are privileged to do many Christlike things, but nothing that we are called upon to do is more Christlike than to forgive.

How, I repeat, did Joseph forgive? First, he was wise enough to keep his hands off God's business. Second, he kept God in the center of his life. What he suffered, therefore, not only did not destroy his faith but served beyond measure to strengthen it.

Keeping God thus at the center, he did not grow sour. No more did he blame God for what he had suffered. He put the blame where it belonged, on the shoulders of his brothers. "You meant it unto evil." He did not forgive by minimizing the sin of his brothers. Jesus did not do so when, on the cross, he prayed for his enemies. When he declared, "They know not what they do," he was not saying that they were not as bad as they seemed, but rather that they were worse.

Refusing to blame God for a wrong in which God was a greater sufferer than himself, he did not ask, "Why should this happen to me?" Really, why did God let Joseph be sold into slavery? There is but one true answer. Because he could not prevent it. God is a king, but he is not a despot. If you choose to hurt somebody, God will not prevent it. But neither will he be defeated by the wrong you do. He will not allow you to get away with that choice. Better still, he will change the evil that you have done into good, provided the one you have wounded will only bear it within the will of God.

Now since Joseph realized that God had not wronged him but that God had suffered with him in his wrong, when he realized further that God was working for good through what he had suffered, he could not grieve this loving God by hating any one of his children. Thus being sure of God, he could give to his cringing brothers a free and full forgiveness.

III

What was the outcome? The author sums it up in this sentence. "The Lord was with Joseph and he prospered." Here is a success story in the finest sense of the word. But the essential fact about this success is not that Joseph, through this grim experience, moved from the tent of a nomad to a palace on the Nile. Though the road of loyalty to God sometimes leads to material success, that is not always the case. Our Lord never promises to pay for our devotion by providing for our physical comfort. "Whatsoever he doeth shall prosper," declares the King James Version of the first psalm. But that is not true. Every good man does not prosper in the sense that he is sure of a place on Easy Street. But what the author really says is, "In whatsoever he does, he shall prosper." His health may fail, his bank may break, but the man himself will still prosper.

24

18212

But it so happens that the prosperity of Joseph was full-orbed. The road that in all reason should have ended in a slave pen ended in a palace. Better still that road led not to the oblivion of a wrecked life but to an immortality of usefulness. Joseph was privileged to save the nation of which he became a part. Even better still he was privileged to save his own people.

Now as a reporter for the *Cairo Courier* I had an interview with Joseph, then an elder statesman honored by both Egyptians and Jews.

"If you will pardon me," I said to this great man, "I should like to ask you just two questions. First, what single event in your life was the most tragic? Of all that you have suffered, what was it that caused the iron so to penetrate your soul that you felt that life was little better than a black despair?"

"I can easily answer that," came the reply. "Far the darkest day that ever broke upon me was that distant day when my own brothers sought to condemn me to a living death by selling me into slavery. I have known no hell hotter than that."

"Thank you," I answered. "There is one other question. What was the most enriching experience you have known through the long years? Having lived in the thick of things, you have known the joy of serving in a big way. But what single event towers above all others?"

"That too is easy," he answers. "Far the best thing that ever happened to me was being sold into slavery. Not only was that my darkest day, but it has become by far the brightest."

25

Thus we see how closely akin was his experience to that of our Lord. What was the worst that the devilish ingenuity of man could do to Jesus? You know the answer; it was to crucify him. Yet that worst has become the very best. But for that lifting up, he would not now, and always, be drawing all men unto himself.

"You meant evil against me," said Joseph, "but God meant it for good." "But God"—those are ever the decisive words. "There they crucified him." How fiendishly final! But God raised him from the dead. Always over and against the worst that man can be and do stands the best that God can be and do. Thus every crucifixion that we suffer for Christ's sake issues in gladsome resurrection.

3

LOYALTY UNLIMITED
—Daniel

"But if not . . ."—Dan. 3:18

■ "But if not"—these are the words of men who are on the road to a more radiant certainty. This is the case because a sense of reality in religion depends most of all upon the fullness of our dedication. It depends upon how far we are willing to go in our loyalty, upon how much we are willing to bet that the faith we profess is really true. Here are three men who grandly venture; therefore, they are able grandly to receive.

The author of the book of Daniel tells this story with a definite purpose. He is speaking to the needs of a desperate day. His nation is a wreck; his people have been scattered over the earth. They are finding today so black that they have lost hope for tomorrow. Therefore, this ancient Barnabas, this son of encouragement, is seeking to bring their dead hopes to a resurrection. This he does, not by putting his accent on what man can do in his own strength but on what God can do in and through man when that man is possessed of loyalty unlimited.

His message, therefore, is as timely as it is timeless. Of

course, we do not face the stark tragedy on the material level that these Jews faced. Instead, we are the most prosperous people that the world has ever known. But while our hands are running over with things, many of our hearts are as empty as a conch shell. This is perhaps the case because too few of us have been loyal to the limit. We have not dared to bet our all that our faith is really true. Maybe then this story of high adventure will help us.

I

The scene is the valley of Dura. It is one of pageantry and splendor. A statue of the king of Babylon is to be unveiled. Everybody who counts for anything is present. There are soldiers, statesmen, the financial and intellectual aristocrats of the nation. The program is very simple. When the Marine Band strikes up the national anthem, everybody is to bow in worship before this statue, which means that they are to worship the king himself.

At the very first note all fall prostrate, each seeking to lie more prone than his neighbor. A field of ripe wheat after personal contact with a steam roller could not have presented a more prosaic flatness. This whole crowd, whatever their ages, was as flexible in their knees as any acrobat. There seems no single exception. But that is a mistake. Three men, Jewish exiles, are still on their feet. Their heads are so far above the clouds that at first they are not seen by the groveling crowd. But such tall men cannot be hidden. They are seen now, and all are sure of their doom. The fury of the king is written on his haughty face.

But to the surprise of all, the blow does not fall at once.

It so happens that this despot, knowing these to be men of integrity and ability, is not willing to throw them away. Therefore, with amazing forbearance, he offers them a second chance, only to have his offer flung back into his royal face.

Here is their mad answer:

We are not going to argue this matter with you. It would be needless since we have already settled the argument in our own hearts. Without any rationalizing, we have decided that what you ask is wrong. We propose, therefore, in spite of your command, to do the will of God, as we are given to see that will. This we do braced by the conviction that God is both able and willing to deliver us out of your hand. We are sure that he will not allow us to suffer so long as we are loyal to his will.

Then something happened that for the moment banished the light from their faces. Perhaps a dirt-eating friend, Simon by name, dared to lift his face far enough from the ground to hiss at them.

Don't be fools! Do you really think that God is able and willing to deliver you out of the king's hand? Do the good always come out on top? Think of the choicest souls among our people. Did every man among them who was loyal without limit escape suffering? Certainly not! Many of them had to pay the last full measure of devotion. Be sensible, therefore. Do as I am doing. The fact that I am groveling here does not mean that I am really worshiping this despot. I am only being prudent. A man must live, you know. What service can he render if he is dead?

II

Then Shadrach, as the spokesman for these three, might have asked their friend this question. "How far are you willing to go in your loyalty to God?" Here is his answer:

I am willing to go as far as the crowd goes. But I am not willing to stand alone. Why should I remain erect when everybody else is bowing? Though a compromise of this kind seems to you at once contemptible and cowardly, yet I cancel out all its ugliness by reminding myself that I am doing nothing more than what others are doing. Everybody is bowing, so why not I?

It is not easy to resist the spell of the crowd. Not long ago I dealt with a bright young teacher who was feeling very strongly the lure of the upward call. But at last he broke off the conversation by saying, "You do not understand. The set in which I move is given to social drinking. I cannot convince myself that this is right, yet if I should refuse to drink with them, I could no longer enjoy their fellowship. Therefore, I am going to stay with my crowd." He would have been glad to have been transformed could he have done so while being conformed to the crowd in which he moved. "I will, if you will is not enough."

2. Then Simon continued, "How far am I willing to go in my loyalty? Just as far as I can without too great a risk to my position, prestige, and power. Of course, I should have gladly stood up with you three, but it would have almost certainly cost me my job."

Years ago a next door neighbor of mine, a worker in his church, ran successfully for office in our city against a gangster government. At once he became the hope of many of our best people, but the very next election he sold out to the foe. When I reminded one of his henchmen of this fact, he replied with a touch of indignation. "Of course, he sold out. Had he refused, he would not have been elected." Integrity was needful, but victory was essential.

What prevented the rich young ruler from becoming a disciple? He felt the spell of Jesus so strongly that he ran after him when nobody else was running, kneeled at his feet when nobody else was kneeling. Yet when Jesus told him how he might have eternal life, this lovable chap turned and went away. When I met him a little later, I dared to say, "Prince, the last time I saw you you were on your knees looking into the face of our Lord inquiring how you might possess eternal life. Did you get what you sought?" "No," he answered, with tragedy looking out from his eyes, "I never got it. I was not willing to pay the price."

Now I can imagine that this groveling friend, who was willing to be loyal on his own terms, might have questioned these brothers with a grudging admiration. "How far are you willing to go in your loyalty to God?" "At first," they answered, "we were willing to go the limit because of our faith that being loyal to God he would not allow us to suffer for our loyalty. We realize now that this is not always the case. Men often suffer for their loyalty. It seems that such is to be our lot. But be that as it may, we purpose to be loyal regardless of cost."

Most of us are professing Christians. Even those who are not often long to be. Almost everybody would like to have a rich, radiant experience of Christ if he could have such on his own terms. But that is not possible. To fix any limit is to fail. To be loyal without limit is to win.

III

What was the cost to these three? At once they were bound and cast into the furnace. Meantime, God never spoke a word. He never lifted a hand. He seemed as indifferent as when his own Son was crucified. How disappointing!

Yet it was hard even for this despot to believe that such high loyalty and courage could go for nothing. He could hardly accept the seeming certainty that these heroic souls were now only a handful of ashes. So he must needs open the door and have a look. This done, he saw not three men but four. The presence of this fourth changed everything. These men, who should have been ashes, were rejoicing in the presence of a mighty companion. The fire had had no power except to burn their fetters and to give them a new awareness of God.

This story is by no means unique. Furnaces for God's saints have been many and varied. But all who experienced these found some kind of deliverance. This is not theory but fact. It is a picture of what has actually taken place times without number. This song was born not of wishful thinking but of actual experience.

> I fear no foe, with Thee at hand to bless;
> Ills have no weight, and tears no bitterness.
> Where is death's sting? where, grave, thy victory?
> I triumph still, if Thou abide with me.

32

So I confront you again with this age-old and ever-new question. How much are you willing to put into the high adventure of being a Christian? If you are satisfied to be partially committed, if you have made up your mind to be limited in your loyalty, then you will miss all that is best in our holy religion. You will experience its prose without any of its poetry. You will know the weight of it without the uplift of its wings. You will be too decent to enjoy sin in its ugly rawness yet not dedicated enough to enjoy the feast of the fullness of life.

In his eagerness to win us to himself, our Lord never minimized the heavy price to be paid. He never sought to conceal the fact that discipleship has a cross red with blood at the very center of it. Having told us that the disciple is to act toward all earthly treasures as if he really hated them, he adds this shocking climax. "Yes and even his own life." That is, nothing will do except loyalty without limit.

There is a sense in which this seems quite harsh. Why is our Lord so demanding? Why is he so insistent that we give our very all? It is certainly not because he is greedy and grasping. He makes these demands because of his infinite eagerness to give his all to us. Here is his own word—"All that I have is thine." What unspeakable wealth that puts within reach of our hands! But how may we receive God's all? In only one way, by giving our all. The hand that is too tightly closed to give is too tightly closed to receive.

Some time ago, while waiting for a plane, I fell into conversation with a stranger. I soon found that he was one of God's saints. He told me of a recent dream that he had had. Now as a rule I find dreams about as exciting as yawns.

But his proved an exception. "I dreamed," he said, "that I had entered the heavenly city. Here my first reaction was not so much one of joy as of wide-eyed wonder at the unbelievable abundance of every spiritual treasure. Looking upon all this infinite wealth, I was ashamed that I had been so poor when I might have been so vastly rich." It is from such an awaking that our Lord is seeking to save us.

Thus, if this unlimited loyalty is costly, it is also vastly rewarding. It is the open road to spiritual certainty. Jesus himself said, "If any man's will is to do his will, he shall know." That means that from whatever point we may start, if we are willing to live up to all the light we have, we shall come to the fullness of the light. That heavenly splendor that blinded Paul might have ended in a deeper darkness but for this one fact: "I was not disobedient to the heavenly vision."

A few years ago, as a pastor, I began to cultivate a bright young husband and father who claimed to be an agnostic. We had some long and earnest conversations. At last he began to come to my church. One day at the close of the sermon, as I was giving the invitation, I saw this chap standing by a pillar far back under the balcony. I then did something that I seldom do; I left the pulpit and approached him personally.

"Jim," I said, "we have talked this over; how about acting on it?"

He turned to the pillar against which he was leaning and said, "I would as soon confess my sins to this pillar as to confess them to Jesus Christ."

"Well," I answered, "we cannot argue that. But I do ask

you one question—are you satisfied with life as you are living it?"

"I am satisfied," he answered.

"That being the case," I replied, "I have nothing more to say."

But as I went back toward the pulpit, my friend was not too far behind. He gave me his hand in token of his acceptance of our Lord. Our friendly people gathered about him with joyful congratulations. But through it all he looked rather glum. When we were alone, he said bluntly, "I'm a stranger to Jesus Christ, I want you to know that. But I want you to know this also; I am willing to do his will at any cost. You told me that that was all he required. I've done what you said, and yet I do not know him."

"That," I replied, "is not only what I said, but it is what Jesus said. Keep facing in that direction, and you certainly will come to know."

His wife told me the remainder of the story. "When we reached home," she said, "Jim amazed me with this question." "Jane, can you pray?" "I'm not too good at it," she replied, "but I'll do my best." "All right," he said, "let's kneel and pray." "But I had uttered only one or two blundering sentences when he took over with an outpouring, not of petition, but of praise." Having been willing to be loyal without limit, he had found a wealth that is also without limit.

4

THE MAN WHO CHOSE
TO SUFFER—*Moses*

"He considered abuse suffered for the Christ greater wealth than the treasures of Egypt."—Heb. 11:26

"And behold, two men talked with him, Moses and Elijah, who appeared in glory and spoke of his departure, which he was to accomplish at Jerusalem."—Luke 9:30-31

■ This daring choice of Moses is separated from this scene on the Mount of Transfiguration by many long centuries. Yet the two are closely related. Indeed, it would be impossible to explain the presence of Moses here apart from that great decision that he had made and reaffirmed so many years before. It was just this choice and the suffering it involved that under God had fitted him for this amazing service on the Mount.

The three synoptic writers agree in carefully fixing the date of this transfiguration scene. It took place one week after our Lord had made his first disclosure of his cross. This, I think, gives a hint of the matter about which Jesus was praying. He was praying here, as he would pray later in Gethsemane, about the exodus that he was soon to accomplish in Jerusalem. He was holding up before his

Father the deep needs of his own soul as he faced that terrible event that, having been accomplished, would enable him to say, "It is finished."

Now I am sure that the coming of these two men, Moses, the great lawgiver and Elijah, one of the greatest of the prophets, was a part of the answer to the prayer of our Lord. Jesus longed intensely for human understanding. He was the loneliest of all lonely men. His was not physical loneliness. That is sometimes hard to bear; in fact it has been known to drive its victim mad. But his was the loneliness of the spirit. It came from seeing a vision that nobody else saw, dreaming great dreams that nobody else shared.

More than once Jesus comforted his lonely heart by the realization that he was understood in the land of light. When, for instance, the scribes and Pharisees sneered at him for receiving sinners, he reminded them that what looked ugly to their eyes was surpassingly beautiful to eyes that saw clearly. He told them that while they might sneer at the turning to God of one of these despised sinners, that in heaven such an event was front-page news. It was something so worthful as to bring joy to the very heart of God.

But this divine understanding did not lessen our Lord's longing for the understanding of his fellows. Over and over he sought to get across to his closest friends something of the meaning of his suffering. But they simply could not understand. "The hour is coming, indeed it has come, when you will be scattered, every man to his home, and will leave me alone." That is the word of a sensitive man who knew himself to be alone and who found loneliness utter agony.

This indicates that the supreme suffering of the Cross

was not physical. Had such been the case, these two great saints would have had little fitness to discuss with our Lord his coming exodus. While Jesus died in great physical agony, Moses and Elijah had known no such experience. It is an arresting and significant fact that these two passed into the unseen with no touch of physical anguish. They seemed to have made their exit as peacefully as a baby falling asleep in his mother's arms. The fitness then of these two men was not born of the fact that they had died in agony, but rather that they had died daily.

Look first at Moses. How has he come upon this holy mountain? It was not a matter of chance or of favoritism. He had reached that sublime height by a long and toilsome road. This journey may be divided into four stages.

I

Moses was born in a slave cabin on the banks of the Nile. He was born under sentence of death. His birth was as lowly as that of our Lord. But while his parents were slaves, they were "in heart and conscience free." They had an overpowering conviction that God had a purpose in the life of this condemned baby.

Gripped by this conviction, they determined that this beautiful baby should live. Therefore, they hid him as long as possible in their own home. Then they took a basket, lined it with pitch and prayer, put him therein, and hid the queer craft among the rushes of the Nile. The daughter of the family, bright little Miriam, was given the task of baby-sitting. It was monotonus enough at first, but soon there was wild excitement. One day she saw a woman, none other than the Princess herself, making her way to the very spot where the little vessel was at anchor. With the Princess were some of her ladies-in-waiting. Upon her arrival at the spot, the baby did what his kind are good at doing. He raised a howl, with the result that his boat was at once discovered and brought to land.

Then it was that this baby changed his craft into a battleship. He laid siege to the heart of the Princess. He cannonaded her with his amazing beauty and with his winsome weakness until she made an unconditional surrender. When watchful Miriam saw the Princess reach her arms for the baby, she knew that the battle had been won.

Then, wise beyond her years, she ran to the Princess and humbly offered to secure a nurse for the child. Given permission, she hurried on winged feet to her mother. Therefore, a little later this wise and eager mother was receiving her own child into her arms, with this haughty command from the Princess: "Take this child away and nurse him for me, and I will give you your wages."

The Princess made a threefold decision that day that was world shaking. She decided that in spite of the king's decree this child should live. Second, she decided that she would adopt him, thus guaranteeing for him the best cultural opportunities of that day. Third, and most important of all, she decided that he was to be nursed by his own mother. That meant that he would be trained in the religion of his own people rather than in the paganism of Egypt.

This choice of the child's own mother to be his nurse was of infinite importance, not simply because she was his mother, but because of the kind of mother she was. She was a woman of vital faith; she was deeply dedicated. Then she was wise enough to know that what was to be done for her child must be done quickly. She could have him with her for only a little while. Soon he would be exposed to the glamorous temptations of a royal court.

Therefore, she told him how God had preserved him in response to her faith. Also that his was a dedicated life, dedicated to the high task of redeeming his people. "Now," she urged, "when you leave us for the palace, you must promise that you will not forget." Since he had caught her contagious faith, he answered solemnly, "I will not forget."

II

Soon the great day came. This young genius passed from a slave's cabin to a royal palace. I can well imagine that he was at first bewildered. But for his faith, which he had learned from his pious parents, he might have had his head turned. His sudden change was more intoxicating than for an obscure actor to become a star overnight. At first the exciting fullness of today drowned out all thought of yesterday. But the impressions made upon him in life's early morning could not be forgotten. Remembering his faith in God, he also remembered his people.

So he paid them a visit. Here he saw an Egyptian bully imposing upon a Hebrew slave. Being of inflammable material, in hot anger he struck the bully dead. I do not think it was his purpose to kill. But though he had taken a life, he was not greatly disturbed. In fact he went back to the palace feeling that he had taken his first step toward ultimate victory. By this blow he would so win the confidence and gratitude of his enslaved people that they would eagerly accept him as their leader.

But soon he saw his mistake. On a second visit, seeing two of his fellow Hebrews striving with each other, he sought to make peace. But instead of accepting his kindly interference, one of them turned on him with a sneer, "Do you mean to kill me as you did that Egyptian?" That shocking word put out every star in Moses' sky. It forced on him the realization that his people were without appreciation, indeed, that they were so sodden in slavery that they did not even desire to be free. Therefore, he took to his heels, not in fear of the wrath of the king (his foster mother could have saved him there), rather he was running from a task that was impossible. He turned away from an evil that, unable to cure, he refused to endure.

III

Then came his long sojourn in the Midian desert. His first days in this wild region were doubtless full of bitter loneliness. He was indeed a stranger in a strange land. He was further tortured by the realization that he had thrown away all the treasures of Egypt to gain nothing better than this drab exile among a handful of rustics. But while thus pitying himself, he could not altogether cease to pity his own people. At times the thought of their wretchedness tortured him. But little by little, in quite a modern fashion, he resorted to certain tranquilizers that enabled him to live with himself.

Here are a few: "I tried to help them, but they did not desire my help. I went to my own, but my own received me not. They thrust me aside. Even God cannot give a people what they will not receive. Certainly, I cannot. I gave up everything for them to win nothing. The fault was not mine but theirs." Thus he prepared himself to go quietly to the end without fulfilling any higher destiny than that of shepherd to another man's sheep.

Then the utterly impossible happened. Glancing from his monotonous task of watching the sheep, he saw a frail bush aflame. It made a very small impression. Soon its gray ashes would be blown away on the desert winds. But when he looked again, the bush was still burning. That gripped his attention. He knew there must be a reason. Therefore, he turned aside, and turning, he heard the voice of God.

"Once you burned like that," said that voice. "You were all aflame with enthusiasm. You were aglow with the high purpose of delivering your people. But now the fire is utterly dead. You even tell yourself that you were a bit of a fool for ever being so hotly interested in what was none of your business."

But this fire that failed to go out had another word for Moses. "What does that frail bush have that you lack?" came the inevitable question. "God" was the answer. "You set yourself to an impossible task. You were going to work deliverance with your own strength, work it with the power that came from the throne of Egypt. Trusting thus in yourself, you made failure inevitable."

"Here," said God, "is another chance. Here you have an opportunity to reaffirm that choice of the long ago. I am going to send you to Egypt. When they ask you this time for your credentials, you will have an answer." Thus with

42

nothing but a staff in his hand and God in his heart, Moses set himself to the accomplishment of one of the greatest achievements of human history.

IV

This final period in the life of Moses was little more than one long trek up Calvary. It was with the utmost difficulty that he was able to shake his sleeping people into wakefulness. It was next to impossible to induce them even to face the land of their hopes. Having at last got them started, it was harder still to keep them going. They were constantly threatening to turn back. They were constant in their fault-finding. Never once did they discover a right thing their great leader had done. They were as devoid of appreciation as the dead.

But in spite of the fact that they were a cantankerous bunch of ungrateful whiners, Moses never gave up. Every day, and all the days, he gave himself wholly to them. Indeed, he carried them in his strong arms across the wilderness as a father might carry a squalling and kicking brat. Then as victory seemed within reach, as he had his foot almost upon the threshold of the land of promise, his great arms went weak, and the howling brat dropped to the ground, still in the wilderness. Thus Moses died without having achieved his purpose. His failure seemed almost as utter and complete as that of Jesus as he went to his cross.

It was this long struggle and seeming failure that helped to fit Moses for his conversation with the Lord about his coming exodus. His dedication, therefore, had not gone for nothing. It brought unspeakable wealth to his own personal life. His own face came to wear the glow of one indwelt by the Spirit. He came also to love with the devotion that made him feel that he could have no heaven for himself unless that heaven could be shared by his own people.

Then he brought to birth a new nation. He helped to make possible the great prophets of Israel. He even had a part in giving to the world this greatest of all:

And in that region there were shepherds out in the field, keeping watch over their flock by night. And an angel of the Lord appeared to them, and the glory of the Lord shone around them, and they were filled with fear. And the angel said to them, "Be not afraid; for behold, I bring you good news of great joy which will come to all the people; for to you is born this day in the city of David a Savior, who is Christ the Lord." (Luke 2:8-11.)

What triumphant failure!

5

I HAVE HAD ENOUGH
—Elijah

"I have had enough of it."—I Kings 19:4 (Moffatt)

"And behold, two men talked with him, Moses and Elijah, who appeared in glory and spoke of his departure, which he was to accomplish at Jerusalem."—Luke 9:30-31

■ No doubt one of the surprises of heaven will be the meeting with certain souls who, in our opinion, had been headed in quite the opposite direction. Even so, we are surprised to meet Elijah on this holy mountain. That Moses, the meekest, the most tamed man of the Old Testament, should be here is not so amazing. But the presence of this bold, drastic, violent prophet is a bit of a shock. Elijah was by nature about as meek as a hungry lion. His favorite weapon in his battle against evil seems to have been a sledge hammer. Yet here we find him in conversation with Moses and our Lord. How did this come about?

I

Of Elijah's background we know almost nothing. We get a glimpse of Moses as a baby. We see Joseph as a youth. But it is hard to imagine that this rugged Puritan was ever either a baby or a teen-ager. Of his father, of his mother, of his teachers we know absolutely nothing. He bursts upon us, not as a sunrise, but rather as the sun in noontide splendor. One moment we do not know of his existence. The next he dashes out of the hills of Gilgal with the violence of a tropical storm.

This tremendous and passionate man was girded by a mighty sense of mission. His people had always been prone to turn aside to the worship of the gods of the nations about them. This proneness to idolatry had been vastly accented by the presence on the throne of Israel of that brilliant and dashing Lady Macbeth, Jezebel. This queen was as fanatical in the promotion of her false religion as she was unscrupulous. Since she completely dominated her royal husband and the court, she was on the way so to dominate the nation as to drive out the religion of Jehovah altogether.

Now the supreme battling force against such tragedy was Elijah. He did not set about his ministry by an appeal to the masses. He began with the classes. His first sermon was not preached in some peasant's cabin but in a royal palace to two royal sinners, Ahab and Jezebel. It was a very short sermon. He did not reason with them. He did not give them their day in court. He rather affirmed their guilt and pronounced sentence against them. There was not to be dew nor rain upon the earth during the coming months except at his word.

Having thus pronounced judgment, with the key to the clouds in his pocket he disappeared into the wilderness. It is not surprising that this denunciation failed to bring the guilty pair to repentance. As they saw their fields become increasingly parched, as they saw their gardens changing into deserts, instead of being softened, they were hardened. Instead of blaming the disease, their rebellion against God, they burned with hate against the physician. Therefore, there was nothing for which these royal sinners longed with such passionate intensity as to destroy this grim and drastic prophet who had dared to rebuke them.

II

Then one day, as suddenly as Elijah had disappeared, he came back. He informed his terrified friend Obediah of his purpose to see Ahab. When this friend told the king of the prophet's return, he heard the news with gleeful rage and at once set out in hot anger to this meeting. Here was just the chance for which he had long been waiting. He was quite sure that he would make this daring preacher cringe. I once saw a dog safe inside his own yard raise his bristles and bare his fangs at a fellow canine on the outside. "I'll tear you limb from limb," he vowed as he dashed toward the gate. But it so happened that somebody opened the gate, and the raging beast became as gentle as a lamb. So it was with Ahab.

"Are you the one who has been troubling Israel?" he inquires with indignation. But the prophet, not the king, dominates the scene. "No," he replied, "I have not troubled Israel, but you and your queen are the real trouble makers, in that you have made Israel to sin." That is the secret of all the real trouble. All our woes come fundamentally from the refusal to do the will of God.

Here Elijah is more reasonable than in his first approach.

47

He received some education at the brook to which God sent him. He had secured yet more in the home of a certain widow who had cared for him graciously. This she had done in spite of the fact that she belonged to the land of Jezebel. He is now, I repeat, willing to give the opposition a hearing. "Let us have a conference," he proposes, "and find out whether God or the Baals can answer with vital fire. That ought to be fair, since they are many, and I am only one."

Ahab could do nothing but agree. So a great throng was gathered on Mount Carmel. To this throng Elijah put a sane question. "How long are you going to cripple yourselves by being divided in your allegiance? Such division can spell nothing but weakness. If God is really God, then serve him. But if Baal be God, serve him. Be wholly for one or wholly for the other."

Then came the test. Elijah gave the priests of Baal the first try. They prayed to their gods from morning to noon without any response. Then came the long afternoon with its shame, defeat, and utter failure. Some of these prophets were doubtless earnest men. They were practicing the religion in which they had been trained. They agonized to the point of blood letting. But nothing happened.

There is something pitiable about their plight. But Elijah had for them not the slightest compassion. He had nothing but scorn and contempt. Here he resorts to the most cruel type of humor—sarcasm. I don't think Elijah ever laughed much. He was not one to "sweeten bitter things with gentle laughter." His humor rather jars upon us as he tells these prophets to cry loud since their gods may be on a journey or just sound asleep. Elijah is desparately in earnest. He

48

is a man of faith. He would have gladly given his body to have been burned in the service of his faith. But he is certainly short on love.

Then came Elijah's turn. There is something majestically moving in his prayer. It was a prayer to which God could respond. The fire did fall. Many half-committed souls began to cry with some degree of conviction, "The Lord is God." It was a kind of revival. However, conversions born of the spectacular are never too impressive. But had the meeting closed then and there, it would have been an occasion of victory.

But sad to say, the final scene is not the falling of the divine fire but the falling of the sword upon the necks of the false prophets. It is one of bloody violence. When the author tells us that Elijah put these false prophets to the sword, I do not believe that he is affirming that the prophet killed them by his own hand. But having preached a gospel more of hate than of love, his followers were living up to the spirit of what he had taught them. If we preach unbrotherliness by our lips and by our lives, sooner or later we shall reap a harvest of violence.

III

The next crisis in the life of this prophet shows a man who has struck bottom. There under the juniper or broom tree he sobs, "I have had enough." His lion-like voice has now become the squeak of a Mickey Mouse as he tells God that he is the only good man alive, and that he hopes that he will not be alive long. Here Elijah died to his self-sufficiency. Here the spikes of crucifixion were driven into his very soul.

What is the matter? This whining was not born of the fact that Elijah was a pessimist. He certainly was not. The first reason for his collapse was that he was utterly exhausted physically. The days before the trial on Carmel had been full of tension. Then when he had won, in wild elation over his victory he had run in front of Ahab's chariot all the way to Jezreel, a distance of 17 miles. From here, not in zest of victory, but in deadly fear, he had gone another day's journey to where he had left his servant. Then there was a final dash into the wilderness where he flung his exhausted body unto this broom tree.

Being thus utterly spent, nervously exhausted, he could no longer see clearly. For the first time, it would seem, in all his stormy life he felt the pangs of loneliness. He had never had a close friend. There had never been a shoulder on which he could lean. He had needed no such support. But here at last, exhausted, seemingly deserted by God and man, he felt terribly alone.

But the bitterest pang of all was his sense of utter defeat and failure. It would be next to impossible to exaggerate the passionate zeal with which he had sought to call the people back to God. But his call had been in vain. "I am no better than my fathers," he sobs. "They allowed the people to go into idolatry. I have been powerless to call them back." As he thus kept books upon himself, he reached the heartbreaking conclusion that his whole stormy life had been no more than a torturing failure. His was a heartache akin to that of John the Baptist, who, with waters of the Dead Sea lapping about his prison, concluded that Jesus was not the Messiah after all, and that his ministry had been no more than a mistake.

IV

The final crisis for Elijah came as he was lodging in a cave at Mount Horeb. God did not rebuke this prophet for his whinning any more than he rebuked John the Baptist. Instead, he gave him a few good, square meals. He also gave him rest. That is always the best and most religious something that a tired person can do. If one is utterly exhausted, he is of little worth to God or man until he gets some rest.

Now having rested and with eyes clearer to see than ever before, God was able to bring him to yet fuller life. This cave scene strikes me as a final step in Elijah's conversion. As this prophet stood in the mouth of the cave, he witnessed a violent storm. Then he felt the thunders of an earthquake. Finally, he thrilled to the wonder of a raging fire. All these were congenial to him. He had been eager for God to do something like this throughout his ministry. Then it came to him as a revelation that God was not in these drastic and violent forces.

Not only were these violent and tremendous forces a revelation to Elijah of the way he thought God ought to act, but they held a mirror up to Elijah himself. Believing that God was a God of violence and of judgment, he, himself, had been a man of violence. He was a stern son of battle. But he was not the kind of man to whom one would have gone with a broken heart. I might gladly have hidden behind him in the face of danger, but I should not have sought his shoulder on which to rest were I suffering from an ill head or a broken heart.

But this vision was not merely negative; it was positive. If God was not in the violent and the drastic, where was he? He was in the voice of gentle stillness. The prophet discovered at last that it is not the noisy that is mighty but the silent. Hate thunders but leaves the heart changed. Love whispers, and a soul is brought to newness of life. Gravity never shrieks, but it holds the planets in its strong fingers. The Cross is not loud, but it is still the supreme magnet of mankind.

From this experience, where Elijah had come to newness of life, he went the last stage of his earthly journey. First, God gave him a friend, Elisha by name. This was the first friend he had ever had. It was in this man's companionship that Elijah did that last heroic mile. It is a thrilling story, worthy of the best in the New Testament. "As they still went on and talked, behold, a chariot of fire and horses of fire separated the two of them. And Elijah went up by a whirlwind into heaven."

Now as this friend watched the departure of Elijah, he shoulted after him these thrilling words. "My father, my father! the chariots of Israel and its horsemen!" There, he declares, goes Israel's standing army. There is a salty soul who, by the giving of himself, has saved his nation from moral disaster.

It is a matter of fine insight that death has no intimate acquaintance with either Moses or Elijah. The grave of Moses was never found. It would seem that Elijah walked right around the headwaters of the river of death without ever so much as a nod to the grave or to the undertaker. Yet so fully did they die to themselves, that with understanding hearts they were able to discuss with our Lord his own coming departure.

6

THE SUFFERING SERVANT

—*Isaiah*

"With his stripes, we are healed."—Isa. 53:5

■ These words are a part of the story of the Suffering Servant. The identity of this servant has been argued for many centuries. In the very early morning of the Christian church an African statesman, having just read the passage of which our text is a part, asked an evangelist, Philip by name, this question: "About whom, pray, does the prophet say this." It was to give a right answer to this seeking soul, I am sure, that Philip had been sent of God to this encounter on the road to Gaza. Here is his reply: "Beginning with this scripture, he told him the good news of Jesus."

Now, if I should dare to follow the example of Philip, I would be in first class company. Not only so, but I would be in the company of the Master himself. "For I tell you," he declared, "this scripture (Isa. 53:12) must be fulfilled in me." (Luke 22:37.) This is not to claim to know all that was in the mind of this prophet. It is not to exclude all reference to ideal Israel. But in my opinion we can be perfectly sure of this, that our Lord regarded himself as this suffering servant.

If further evidence is needed, here are two facts, I think, upon which most of us can agree. First, this passage does describe the Man who walks through the pages of the Gospels with such an amazing accuracy as to be beyond all merely human achievement. We are sure that no man could have so written except under the inspiration of the Holy Spirit. Second, not only does this passage describe our Lord with unbelievable accuracy, but it does not so describe any other group or individual that ever lived. Put this royal robe about the shoulders of any man except Jesus, and the result would be far more grotesque than when King Saul tried to fit his armor to youthful David. That is, this picture of the Suffering Servant does describe our Lord as it describes no other individual or group.

I

Isaiah tells us something of the lowly origin of this suffering servant and of the reception that he met at the hands of men. "He grew up before him like a young plant," like a shoot from a tree that had been cut down. He was "like a root out of dry ground." He did not have the impressiveness of a tree planted by a river. His origin was as surprising as the fact that a peasant woman in a lowly stable could hold the Word made flesh in her arms.

As to his reception, by the big world he was utterly ignored. Of the millions living at the date of his birth, almost nobody knew that anything out of the ordinary had happened. While a little handful in his own land were compelled to take knowledge of his presence, while an insignificant few believed in him and loved him, by the vast majority "he was despised and rejected." While some looked at him with a touch of wistful perplexity in their eyes, others looked on him with contempt.

By and by this contempt issued in bitter hatred and violence. There was a little handful of priestly politicians who saw in him a threat to their prestige and power. Therefore, they resolved to be rid of him at all cost.

This Prophet does not tell us how the servant was killed. He makes no specific mention of the Cross. But what is more important, he tells us how the Cross came to be. "By oppression and judgment he was taken away." That is, his death was a miscarriage of justice. His was a judicial murder. Though Pilate had more than once declared him not guilty, he at last sentenced him to die on a cross. Thus whenever we recite our creed, we remind ourselves of this judicial murder. "He suffered under Pontius Pilate."

Not only did he die unjustly, but his death had for the men of his day no adequate meaning. Some thought he was "smitten of God," that he was suffering for his own sin. But nobody understood. "Who considered that he was . . . stricken for the transgression of my people." The only answer is, nobody. When Jesus breathed his last upon the Cross, there was not one single soul in all the world who understood the meaning and purpose of his death. This was the case not only with his foes but with his friends as well.

II

What is the meaning of this death? Why did God allow this suffering servant thus to die? The answer given by this prophet is shocking. "Yet it was the will of God to bruise him." That is, this judicial murder took place within the will of God. In saying this, the prophet is in complete harmony with the New Testament (Acts 4:27-28). But we are not to understand by this that it was the will of God that men should hate and reject our Lord. He willed the exact opposite. But since they did hate and reject him, it was his will that the servant should die for their redemption.

Not only was this death the will of God, but it was also the will of Jesus himself. When he offered his first prayer in Gethsemane, he still had hope that there might be some other way. "My Father, if it be possible, let this cup pass from me." But while he deeply dreaded the cross, he dreaded failure to do the will of God far more. Therefore, he added, "Nevertheless, not as I will, but as thou wilt." Having thus prayed, the will of God became clear. Therefore, his next prayer is one of acceptance: "If this cannot pass unless I drink it, thy will be done."

Therefore, this legal murder, I repeat, did not only take place within the will of God but within the will of Jesus as well. The prophet says, "He makes himself an offering for sin." Here is the Good Shepherd laying down his life for the sheep. If God so loved the world that he gave his only begotten son, even so the Son so loved the world that he gave himself. Thus Isaiah says what Jesus confirmed. He suffered to make us whole. It is by his wounds that we have been healed.

III

Now this healing that has been made available for us at such infinite cost certainly implies that we are in need of healing. Ours is a sick world, a sick society. This is the case because we are sick individually. If that is not the case, then all God's efforts, culminating in Calvary, fail to make sense.

Many years ago a half-wit who lived some two miles from our village dashed to the door of our local physician, shouting that his mother was dying. Now in those days a doctor's reputation depended very largerly upon the quickness of his action. Therefore, this good man sprang upon his horse and rode at frantic speed to the home of the dying woman, only to find her quietly sweeping the yard. Of course, he looked silly. He had acted upon the word of an idiot.

Our sickness is a reality. It is a sickness born of sin. Sin separates from God the source of all health and life. We need this healing, said the Prophet, because we have gone astray. What is it to go astray? A stray sheep is not necessarily a bad sheep. His whole tragedy is summed up in the fact that he has turned to his own way. Having done this, he no longer follows the shepherd.

Here we come to the fountain source of all wrong doing. It is not merely to do cruel and vicious things of set purpose. It is simply doing our own will, turning to our way instead of God's way. I well remember the first time, as a small boy, I ever left home without the knowledge and consent of my father and mother. I followed the wagon of a colored man who was moving to a house on our farm. Having arrived at said house, the first object unloaded was a Negro boy about my own age. Then came a homemade wagon.

We took turn about pulling each other, and the day passed like a dream.

Meantime, without any thought of doing so, I was causing quite a bit of anxiety at home. Nobody had the slightest idea where the young prodigal had gone. The other members of the family set out in different directions seeking me. At last one of my brothers found me, and we went home in a kind of triumphant procession. They were all glad to see me. But if you think my father killed the fatted calf, you are mistaken. Instead, he wisely offered up the prodigal. Yet I did not mean any harm at all. I had just turned to my own way.

Now the fact that this going of our own way is back of all sin does not mean that all who turn to their own way will reach the same goal. The elder son who remained slavishly at home refused to claim kin with his prodigal brother. But in so doing, he was wrong. Why did the prodigal go away?— not to hurt anybody, but to please himself. Why did his brother stay at home?—not to help anybody, but also to please himself. Thus they were blood brothers after all.

It is not the differing goals to which self-will leads that are really significant; it is rather the common motive that lies back of our reaching those goals. One man can make self-pleasing the law of his life and win a fortune, while another can live by the same law and go broke. One by turning to his own way can end on a scaffold, while another can do the same and end on the platform of a popular pulpit. It is not, I repeat, the differing goals that count but the common motive that lies back of these goals.

Now every man who turns to his own way becomes

59

spiritually sick. This sickness is a source of weakness. In its grip we find ourselves without sufficient strength to do the right, also too weak to resist the wrong. We are often fretful and feverish, having spurned the will of God in which alone is our peace. Instead of being assets we too often become liabilities. We thus become a drag upon others, making it harder for them to do the right and easier for them to do the wrong.

IV

For this sickness Isaiah tells us there is a remedy. "With his stripes we are healed." That is also the conviction of the writers of the New Testament. It is a conviction that has been strengthened and kept fresh and vital by experience. Our Lord confronts us today, as he has confronted countless thousands of beaten men and women, with the same question that he put to a hopeless wreck long centuries ago: "Do you want to be healed?" This is to assert not only that this poor chap is sick, but also that he can be made well. If such is not the case, the question is not kindly but devilish.

Now if he is to be healed, how is it to come about? How may this worthless bit of wreckage become worthful? How, having lain flat of his back for half a lifetime, can he stand once more upon his feet? How can he be made whole? That is of deep interest. Today I think we appreciate good health as never before. When I was a boy, it was hardly good form to be entirely well, especially physically. "Tolerable" was about as much as anybody dared to claim. But we have learned better. Almost all of us would like to be every whit whole.

When you consult a physician in quest of this goal, what do you have in mind? Unless you are a trifler, you expect to put yourself in some meaure in his hands. If you have no intention of doing what he says, then your consulting is mere costly nonsense. Did you ever undergo surgery? What an adventure of faith that is! To go to sleep in the hands of a mere man, knowing that one false move on his part might cost you your life, that is faith to a high degree. Yet multitudes of us have so dared, knowing that the best physicians sometimes fail.

How much easier it ought to be for us to put ourselves in the hands of that Physician who never fails. "By his wounds we have been healed." Our part is to accept this healing that may be ours without money and without price. Isaiah was sure that many would do just that. "He shall see the fruit of the travail of his soul and be satisfied." Thus he affirmed with Jesus that, lifted up from the earth, he would draw all men unto himself.

How much will it take to satisfy our Lord? It would be presumptuous of me to seek to give a full answer to that question. But I am perfectly sure of this; he will never be satisfied in time or eternity until we turn to him for healing. We can bring him that satisfaction at this moment. When a healthy baby is born, the mother is satisfied, both because of what he is and of what he may become. If we turn to Christ today, he will be satisfied with us now with a satisfaction that, if we continue in our loyalty, will go on growing throughout eternity.

"Beginning with this scripture he told him the good news of Jesus." So what? It made a difference then and there to the Secretary of the Treasury for Ethiopia. His perplexity gave way to certainty. "And he went on his way rejoicing." May God grant that the reading of this same good news may have a like happy ending for every one of us!

Date Due

DEC 3 '63	MAY 15 '68	4~11	
MAR 31 '64	MAY 29 '68	OCT 19 '76	
Sept. 3'64	MAR 7 '69	APR 18 '77	
SEP 14 '64	MAY 22 '69	JUN 7 '76	
DEC 1 '64	NOV 12 '69	APR 8 '80	
FEB 1 '65	NOV 26 '69	3.19.81	
MAR 20 '65	MAR 19 '70	MAY 15 '81	
MAR 5 '66	APR 2 '70	OCT 27 '82	
APR 15 '66	SEP 30 '70	APR 13 '83	
OCT 8 '66	NOV 17 '70	NOV 14 '84	
NOV 8 '66	NOV 30 '70	DEC 19 '84	
DEC 1 '67	DEC 14 '70	JAN 23 '85	
JAN 17 '97	MAR 18 '71		
MAR 29 '67	APR 15 '71		
Sept 5	NOV 24 '71		
APR 16 '68	DEC 8 '71		
APR 30 '68	MAR 2 '72		
	MAR 2 '72		